I Believe
GOD LOVES ME

Revealing God's Love For All
People Through Scripture

Terry Rich

D1468937

I Believe

God Loves Me

If you have more questions about God, please visit
www.GotQuestions.org

Go to www.peacefulheartjournal.com
to download this booklet for free or to
read the next booklet in this series called -
I Believe I AM

All images are courtesy of Canva.com and
UnSplash.com

TABLE OF CONTENTS

36 God can do more than I can possibly imagine
37 I am valuable to God
38 God comforts me in all my troubles
39 God is close to me
40 God cares for me with tenderness
41 In Jesus, God reveals himself to me
42 I can see God through the life of Jesus
43 God will do anything for me
44 God sees me and welcomes be back
45 Jesus died to show how much God loves me
46 Jesus restores my relationship with God
47 God embraces me when I believe in Jesus
48 God is my closest friend
49 Nothing will ever separate me from God again
50 God celebrates when I believe
51 My true father is God
52 When I become God's child, I have a new life
53 All mankind long for eternity
54 In eternity, God will take away all suffering
55 God has a place prepared for me in Heaven
56 My everlasting life begins now
57 I have a fresh start with God beside me
58 My new heart and spirit can relate to God
59 When I follow Jesus my life is satisfying
60 I can be free from fear and have God's peace
61 I trust God and depend on Him
62 I have reason to praise
63 Love is God's number #1 priority
64 The world needs Gods love
65 God's love flows right through me

A WORD FROM LONG AGO ...

Acts 17:22-28

So Paul [*the apostle of Jesus*], standing before them at the Mars Hill forum, addressed them as follows:

"Men of Athens [*the world*], I notice that you are very religious, for as I was out walking I saw your many altars, and one of them had this inscription on it — 'To the Unknown God.' You have been worshiping Him without knowing who He is, and now I wish to tell you about Him. He made the world and everything in it, and since He is Lord of heaven and earth, He doesn't live in man-made temples; and human hands can't minister to His needs—for He has no needs! He himself gives life and breath to everything, and satisfies every need there is. He created all the people of the world from one man, Adam, and scattered the nations across the face of the earth. He decided beforehand which should rise and fall, and when. He determined their boundaries. His purpose in all of this is that they should seek after God, and perhaps feel their way toward Him and find Him—though He is not far from any one of us. For in Him we live and move and are! As one of your own poets says it, 'We are the sons of God.'

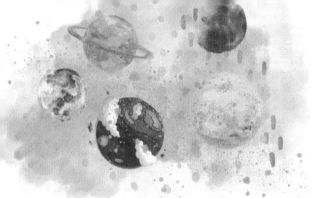

GOD CREATED EVERYTHING

In the beginning God created the Heavens and Earth—all you see, all you don't see.

Genesis 1:1

EVERYTHING WAS CREATED JUST FOR GOD

For by Him all things were created, in heaven and on earth, visible and invisible, whether thrones or dominions or rulers or authorities—all things were created through Him and for Him.

Colossians 1:16

GOD CREATED ME

God created human beings in His image, reflecting God's nature. He created them male and female.

Genesis 1:27

GOD GAVE MAN A PERFECT PLACE TO LIVE

And God planted a garden in Eden, in the east, and there He put the man whom He had formed. God placed the man in the Garden of Eden as its gardener, to tend and care for it.

Genesis 2:8,15

GOD GAVE MAN ONE RULE TO SHOW HE REIGNS

God warned "the tree of the knowledge of good and evil you shall not eat, for in the day that you eat of it you shall surely die".

Genesis 2:17

MAN DISOBEYED GOD BECAUSE OF SELFISH DESIRE

When the woman saw that
the tree looked like good
eating and realized what she
would get out of it—she'd
know everything!—she took
and ate the fruit and then
gave some to her husband,
and he ate.

Genesis 3:6

THE RELATIONSHIP BETWEEN GOD & MAN WAS BROKEN

When they heard the sound of God strolling in the garden in the evening breeze, the man and his wife hid in the trees of the garden, they hid from God.

Genesis 3:8

MAN NATURALLY WANTS HIS OWN WAY, NOT GOD'S

When Adam sinned,
sin entered the entire
human race. His sin
spread death throughout
all the world, so
everything began
to grow old and die,
for all sinned.

Romans 5:12

GOD CHOSE ME WHEN HE PLANNED CREATION

Because of what Christ has done, we have become gifts to God that he delights in, for as part of God's sovereign plan we were chosen from the beginning to be His, and all things happen just as He decided long ago.

Ephesians 1:11

15

GOD KNEW ME EVEN BEFORE I WAS CONCEIVED

Before I shaped you in the womb, I knew all about you. Before you saw the light of day, I had plans for you.

Jeremiah 1:5

GOD KNIT ME TOGETHER IN MY MOTHER'S WOMB

God made all the delicate, inner parts of my body and knit them together in my mother's womb.

Psalm 139:13

GOD DECIDED MY BIRTH AND WHERE I WOULD LIVE

He created all the people of the world from one man, Adam, and scattered the nations across the face of the earth. He decided beforehand which should rise and fall, and when. He determined their boundaries.

Acts 17:26

GOD BREATHED LIFE INTO ME

The God who created the cosmos, stretched out the skies, laid out the earth and all that grows from it, who breathes life into earth's people, makes them alive with His own life.

Isaiah 42:5

19

GOD PLANNED OUT ALL MY DAYS

You saw me before I was born and scheduled each day of my life before I began to breathe. Every day was recorded in your book!

Psalm 139:16

GOD HAS BEEN WITH ME SINCE THE DAY I WAS BORN

Yes, you God have been with me from birth and have helped me constantly.

Psalm 71:6

GOD MADE ME TO BE MARVELOUS, A TRUE WORK OF ART

Thank you for making me so wonderfully complex! It is amazing to think about. Your workmanship is marvelous—and how well I know it.

Psalm 139:14

22

GOD DEARLY LOVES ME

We know how much
God loves us because
we have felt His love
and because we believe
Him when he tells us
that He loves us dearly.
God is love.

1 John 4:16

GOD CALLS ME HIS CHILD AND HE IS MY FATHER

What marvelous love
the Father has extended
to us! Just look at it—
we're called children of
God! That's who
we really are.

1 John 3:1

GOD OFFERS MORE THAN MY EARTHLY FATHER EVER COULD

And if you hard-hearted, sinful men know how to give good gifts to your children, won't your Father in heaven even more certainly give good gifts to those who ask Him for them?

Matthew 7:11

EVERY GOOD THING I HAVE COMES FROM GOD

But whatever is good
and perfect comes to
us from God,
the Creator of all light,
and He shines
forever without
change or shadow.

James 1:17

GOD WILL PROVIDE FOR ALL MY NEEDS

Therefore I tell you, do
not be anxious about your life,
what you will eat or what you
will drink, nor about your body,
what you will put on. Is not life
more than food, and the body
more than clothing. Look at the
birds of the air: they neither sow
nor reap nor gather into barns,
and yet your heavenly Father
feeds them. Are you not
of more value than they?

Matthew 6:25-27

27

GOD'S PLAN FOR MY FUTURE IS FILLED WITH HOPE

For I know the plans I have for you, says the Lord. They are plans for good and not for evil, to give you a future and a hope.

Jeremiah 29:11

GOD'S LOVE FOR ME NEVER ENDS

Oh, give thanks to the Lord, for He is good; His loving-kindness continues forever.

Psalm 139:1

GOD THINKS ABOUT ME CONSTANTLY

How precious it is, Lord, to realize that You are thinking about me constantly! I can't even count how many times a day Your thoughts turn toward me. And when I waken in the morning, You are still thinking of me! I can't even count how many times a day Your thoughts turn toward me. And when I waken in the morning, You are still thinking of me!

Psalm 139:17-18

GOD REJOICES OVER ME

God will rejoice over you
with great gladness;
He will love you and
not accuse you. Is that a
joyous choir I hear? No,
it is the Lord himself
exulting over you
in happy song.

Zephaniah 3:17

31

GOD'S GOODNESS SURROUNDS ME

He is good to everyone,
and His compassion is
intertwined with
everything He does.

Psalm 145:9

GOD WANTS TO SHOW ME GREAT THINGS

Call to Me and I will answer you. I'll tell you marvelous and wondrous things that you could never figure out on your own.

Jeremiah 33:3

WHEN I SEEK GOD, HE IS THERE

If you seek God, you'll be able to find Him if you're serious, looking for Him with your whole heart and soul.

Deuteronomy 4:29

GOD WANTS TO GIVE ME MY HEART'S DESIRES

Seek your happiness in the Lord. Then He will give you all your heart's desires.

Psalm 37:4

GOD CAN DO MORE THAN I CAN POSSIBLY IMAGINE

Now glory be to God, who by His mighty power at work within us is able to do far more than we would ever dare to ask or even dream of—infinitely beyond our highest prayers, desires, thoughts, or hopes.

Ephesians 3:20

I AM VALUABLE TO GOD

What is the price of five sparrows? A couple of pennies? Not much more than that. Yet God does not forget a single one of them. And he knows the number of hairs on your head! Never fear, you are far more valuable to Him than a whole flock of sparrows.

Luke 12:6-7

GOD COMFORTS ME IN ALL MY TROUBLES

What a wonderful God we have—He is the Father of our Lord Jesus Christ, the source of every mercy, and the One who so wonderfully comforts and strengthens us in our hardships and trials.

2 Corinthians 1:3-4

GOD IS CLOSE TO ME

If your heart is broken, you'll find God right there; if you're kicked in the gut, He'll help you catch your breath.

Psalm 34:18

GOD CARES FOR ME WITH TENDERNESS

Like a shepherd, God will care for His flock, gathering the lambs in His arms, Hugging them as He carries them, leading the nursing ewes to good pasture.

Isaiah 40:11

IN JESUS, GOD REVEALS HIMSELF TO ME

God has made Christ's very being known to them—who He is and what He does—and continues to make it known, so that God's love for Christ might be in them.

John 17:26

I CAN SEE GOD THROUGH THE LIFE OF JESUS

This Son perfectly
mirrors God,
and is stamped
with God's nature.
He holds everything
together by what
He says—
powerful words!

Hebrews 1:3

GOD WILL DO ANYTHING FOR ME

With God on our side like
this, how can we lose?
If God didn't hesitate to put
everything on the line for us,
embracing our condition and
exposing Himself to the
worst by sending His own
Son to die, is there anything
else He wouldn't gladly
and freely do for us?

Romans 8:31

GOD SEES ME AND WELCOMES ME BACK

So he got up and returned to his father. But while he was still a long way off, his father saw him and felt compassion for him, and ran and embraced him and kissed him.

Luke 15:20

JESUS DIED TO SHOW HOW MUCH GOD LOVES ME

This is how God showed his love for us: God sent His only Son into the world so we might live through Him. This is the kind of love we are talking about—not that we once upon a time loved God, but that He loved us and sent his Son as a sacrifice to clear away our sins and the damage they've done to our relationship with God.

1 John 4:10

JESUS RESTORES MY RELATIONSHIP WITH GOD

God who brought us back to Himself through what Christ Jesus did. And God has given us the privilege of urging everyone to come into His favor and be reconciled to Him. For God was in Christ, restoring the world to Himself, no longer counting men's sins against them but blotting them out.

2 Corinthians 5:18-19

GOD EMBRACES ME WHEN I BELIEVE IN JESUS

No one who denies the Son has any part with the Father, but affirming the Son is an embrace of the Father as well.

1 John 2:23

JESUS IS MY CLOSEST FRIEND

You were His enemies and hated Him and were separated from Him by your disobedient thoughts and actions, yet now He has brought you back as His friends. He has done this through the death on the cross of His own human body, and now as a result Christ has brought you into the very presence of God, and you are standing there before Him with nothing left against you.

Colossians 1:21-23

NOTHING WILL EVER SEPARATE ME FROM GOD AGAIN

Nothing can ever separate us from God's love. Death can't, and life can't. The angels won't, and all the powers of hell itself cannot keep God's love away. Our fears for today, our worries about tomorrow, or where we are—high above the sky, or in the deepest ocean—nothing will ever be able to separate us from the love of God demonstrated by our Lord Jesus Christ when He died for us.

Romans 8:38-39

GOD
CELEBRATES
WHEN I BELIEVE

Count on it—there's
more joy in heaven over
one sinner's rescued life
than over ninety-nine
good people in no
need of rescue.

Luke 15:7

MY TRUE FATHER IS GOD

No one else should carry the title of 'Father'; you have only one Father, and He's in heaven.

Matthew 23:9

WHEN I BECOME GOD'S CHILD, I HAVE A NEW LIFE

But to all who received Christ, He gave the right to become children of God. All they needed to do was to trust Him to save them. All those who believe this are reborn!—not a physical rebirth resulting from human passion or plan— but from the will of God.

John 1:12-13

ALL MANKIND LONG FOR ETERNITY

God has planted eternity in the hearts of men, even so, many cannot see the whole scope of God's work from beginning to end.

Ecclesiastes 3:11

IN ETERNITY, GOD WILL TAKE AWAY ALL SUFFERING

I heard a loud shout from the throne saying, "Look, the home of God is now among men, and He will live with them and they will be His people; yes, God Himself will be among them. He will wipe away all tears from their eyes, and there shall be no more death, nor sorrow, nor crying, nor pain. All of that has gone forever."

Revelation 21:3-4

GOD HAS A PLACE PREPARED FOR ME IN HEAVEN

There are many homes up there where my Father lives, and I am going to prepare them for your coming. When everything is ready, then I will come and get you, so that you can always be with Me where I am.

John 14:2-3

MY EVERLASTING LIFE BEGINS NOW

It is God who saved us and chose us for His holy work not because we deserved it but because that was His plan long before the world began— to show His love and kindness to us through Christ.
And now He has made all of this plain to us by the coming of our Savior Jesus Christ, who broke the power of death and showed us the way of everlasting life through trusting Him.

2 Timothy 1:9-10

I HAVE A FRESH START WITH GOD BESIDE ME

When someone becomes a Christian, he becomes a brand new person inside. He is not the same anymore. A new life has begun!

2 Corinthians 5:17

MY NEW HEART AND SPIRIT CAN RELATE TO GOD

And I will give you a new heart, and a new spirit I will put within you. And I will remove the heart of stone from your flesh and give you a heart of flesh.

Ezekiel 36:26

WHEN I FOLLOW JESUS MY LIFE IS SATISFYING

Jesus said "I am the Gate for the sheep, all others who came before me were thieves and robbers. But the true sheep did not listen to them. Yes, I am the Gate. Those who come in by way of the Gate will be saved and will go in and out and find green pastures. The thief's purpose is to steal, kill and destroy.
My purpose is to give life in all its fullness.

John 10:7-10

I CAN BE FREE FROM FEAR AND HAVE GOD'S PEACE

Peace I leave with you; My peace I give to you. Not as the world gives do I give to you. Let not your hearts be troubled, neither let them be afraid.

John 14:27

I TRUST GOD AND DEPEND ON HIM

You can never please God without faith, without depending on Him. Anyone who wants to come to God must believe that there is a God and that He rewards those who sincerely look for him.

Hebrews 11:6

I HAVE REASON TO PRAISE

God's proved he's on my side; I've thrown my lot in with him. Now I'm jumping for joy, and shouting and singing my thanks to Him.

Psalm 28:7

LOVE IS GOD'S NUMBER #1 PRIORITY

Jesus replied, 'Love the Lord your God with all your heart, soul, and mind.' This is the first and greatest commandment. The second most important is similar: 'Love your neighbor as much as you love yourself.'

Matthew 22:37-38

THE WORLD NEEDS GODS LOVE

Let us continue to love each other since love comes from God. Everyone who loves is born of God and experiences a relationship with God. The person who refuses to love doesn't know the first thing about God, because God is love—so you can't know Him if you don't love.

1 John 4:7-8

GOD'S LOVE FLOWS RIGHT THROUGH ME

Watch what God does, and then you do it, like children who learn proper behavior from their parents. Mostly what God does is love you. Keep company with Him and learn a life of love. Observe how Christ loved us. His love was not cautious but extravagant. He didn't love in order to get something from us but to give everything of Himself to us. Love like that.

Ephesians 5:1-2

AS SPOKEN FROM LONG AGO …

Are you ready to become one of the "Sons of God"?

Do you believe that your purpose in all of this is that you should seek after God, find your way toward Him and truly find Him?

If so, then choose now to believe that Jesus Christ is your Savior, the One who shed His blood on the cross so that your relationship with God can be restored!

**Are you ready to
choose to believe …**

God Loves You?

If you have more questions about God, please visit
www.GotQuestions.org

Go to www.peacefulheartjournal.com
**to download this booklet for free or to
read the next booklet in this series called -
I Believe I AM**

Notes:

Notes:

Notes:

Notes:

Notes:

Notes:

Notes:

Notes:

Notes:

Notes:

Notes:

Notes:

Notes:

Notes:

Notes:

Notes:

Notes:

Notes:

Made in the USA
Middletown, DE
04 July 2022